FOR THE BLACK LEADER & BUSINESSMAN
RISE UP

INTRODUCTION

IN THE PAGES THAT FOLLOW, YOU WILL FIND A COLLECTION OF ENCOURAGEMENT, REMINDERS, AND PRACTICAL ADVICE DESIGNED TO UPLIFT AND EMPOWER YOU ON YOUR JOURNEY. WHETHER YOU ARE A YOUNG MAN JUST STARTING OUT, OR A SEASONED PROFESSIONAL LOOKING TO MAKE A GREATER IMPACT, THIS BOOK IS FOR YOU.

EMBRACE YOUR POWER, HONOR YOUR POTENTIAL, AND DARE TO THINK BIG. TOGETHER, LET US RISE ABOVE LIMITATIONS, DEFY EXPECTATIONS, AND CREATE A WORLD WHERE EVERY BLACK MAN HAS THE OPPORTUNITY TO LEAD AND THRIVE.

A SPECIAL MENTION TO CKT SOLUTIONS LTD
DEDICATED TO SPREADING AWARENESS ON THE IMPORTANCE OF CREATING TOMORROW'S FUTURE BLACK LEADERS & ENTREPRENUERS, NOW.

THIS BOOK CONTAINS:
X6 INSPIRING CASE STUDIES
X9 STRONG AFFIRMATIONS
X90 QUOTES FOR X90 DAY EMPOWERMENT

YESTERDAY - NOW - TOMMOROW

RISE UP

CASE STUDY

MARCUS GARVEY

BACKGROUND:
MARCUS MOSIAH GARVEY, BORN ON AUGUST 17, 1887, IN ST. ANN'S BAY, JAMAICA, EMERGED AS A PROMINENT FIGURE IN THE EARLY 20TH-CENTURY BLACK NATIONALIST AND PAN-AFRICAN MOVEMENTS. INFLUENCED BY THE RACIAL DISPARITIES HE WITNESSED IN JAMAICA AND LATER IN THE UNITED STATES, GARVEY DEDICATED HIMSELF TO UPLIFTING PEOPLE OF AFRICAN DESCENT.

SUCCESS STORY:
GARVEY'S MOST NOTABLE SUCCESS WAS THE ESTABLISHMENT OF THE BLACK STAR LINE IN 1919. THIS SHIPPING COMPANY AIMED TO FACILITATE TRADE AND COMMUNICATION AMONG BLACK COMMUNITIES WORLDWIDE, SYMBOLIZING GARVEY'S VISION OF ECONOMIC INDEPENDENCE. WHILE THE BLACK STAR LINE FACED FINANCIAL CHALLENGES AND EVENTUAL FAILURE, ITS CREATION MARKED A SIGNIFICANT ACHIEVEMENT IN GARVEY'S MISSION TO FOSTER ECONOMIC AUTONOMY WITHIN THE BLACK COMMUNITY.
GARVEY'S SUCCESS EXTENDED BEYOND THE UNITED STATES, AS THE UNIA BECAME A GLOBAL MOVEMENT, ATTRACTING MILLIONS OF FOLLOWERS. HIS POWERFUL ORATORY SKILLS AND VISION FOR A UNITED AFRICAN DIASPORA RESONATED WITH PEOPLE IN THE CARIBBEAN, AFRICA, AND EUROPE. DESPITE LEGAL CHALLENGES AND IMPRISONMENT, GARVEY'S IDEAS LEFT AN ENDURING LEGACY, INFLUENCING SUBSEQUENT CIVIL RIGHTS LEADERS AND PAN-AFRICAN MOVEMENTS.

YESTERDAY · NOW · TOMMOROW

RISE UP

AFFIRMATION

"I TRUST MY INSTINCTS AND MAKE DECISIONS THAT ALIGN WITH MY VALUES AND VISION."

RISE UP

QUOTE

"WHEN I DARE TO BE POWERFUL, TO USE MY STRENGTH IN THE SERVICE OF MY VISION, THEN IT BECOMES LESS AND LESS IMPORTANT WHETHER I AM AFRAID."
— AUDRE LORDE

RISE UP

QUOTE

"KNOWLEDGE IS THE CURRENCY OF SUCCESS. AS A BLACK ENTREPRENEUR, NEVER STOP INVESTING IN YOUR EDUCATION."
- BYRON ALLEN

RISE UP

QUOTE

"WHEN YOU ARE DECIDING ON NEXT STEPS, NEXT JOBS, NEXT CAREERS, FURTHER EDUCATION, YOU SHOULD RATHER FIND PURPOSE THAN A JOB OR A CAREER. PURPOSE CROSSES DISCIPLINES. PURPOSE IS AN ESSENTIAL ELEMENT OF YOU. IT IS THE REASON YOU ARE ON THE PLANET AT THIS PARTICULAR TIME IN HISTORY."
- CHADWICK BOSEMAN

RISE UP

QUOTE

"YOU CAN AND SHOULD SET YOUR OWN LIMITS AND CLEARLY ARTICULATE THEM. THIS TAKES COURAGE, BUT IT IS ALSO LIBERATING AND EMPOWERING, AND OFTEN EARNS YOU NEW RESPECT."
— ROSALIND BREWER

RISE UP

QUOTE

"SUCCESS IS LIKING YOURSELF, LIKING WHAT YOU DO, AND LIKING
HOW YOU DO IT."
- MAYA ANGELOU

RISE UP

QUOTE

"THE ROAD BACK MAY NOT BE AS SHORT AS WE WISH,... BUT THERE ARE SOLID REASONS TO FEEL CONFIDENT ABOUT THE FUTURE."
— RICHARD PARSONS

RISE UP

QUOTE

"THE MORE YOU LEARN, THE MORE YOU EARN. AS BLACK ENTREPRENEURS, KNOWLEDGE IS OUR GREATEST ASSET."
- SARAH BREEDLOVE (MADAM C.J. WALKER)

RISE UP

QUOTE

"SUCCESS IS TO BE MEASURED NOT SO MUCH BY THE POSITION THAT ONE HAS REACHED IN LIFE AS BY THE OBSTACLES WHICH HE HAS OVERCOME WHILE TRYING TO SUCCEED."
— BOOKER T. WASHINGTON

RISE UP

QUOTE

"HAVE A VISION. BE DEMANDING."
— COLIN POWELL

RISE UP

QUOTE

"STARTING MY OWN BUSINESS WAS THE FIRST STEP TOWARDS TAKING CONTROL OF MY DESTINY."
- TYLER PERRY

YESTERDAY · NOW · TOMMOROW

RISE UP

QUOTE

"NEVER EVER CHASE MONEY. YOU SHOULD CHASE SUCCESS,
BECAUSE WITH SUCCESS MONEY FOLLOWS."
— WILFRED EMMANUEL-JONES

RISE UP

QUOTE

"THE BIGGEST RISK IN LIFE IS NOT TAKING ANY RISK AT ALL.
AS BLACK ENTREPRENEURS, WE MUST BE BOLD AND TAKE ACTION."
- ROBERT L. JOHNSON

RISE UP

QUOTE

"SUCCESS ISN'T ABOUT HOW MUCH MONEY YOU MAKE; IT'S ABOUT THE DIFFERENCE YOU MAKE IN PEOPLE'S LIVES."
— MICHELLE OBAMA

RISE UP

CASE STUDY

MUHAMMAD ALI

BACKGROUND:

MUHAMMAD ALI, BORN CASSIUS MARCELLUS CLAY JR. ON JANUARY 17, 1942, IN LOUISVILLE, KENTUCKY, WAS AN AMERICAN PROFESSIONAL BOXER, CULTURAL ICON, AND PHILANTHROPIST. GROWING UP IN THE SEGREGATED SOUTH, ALI DEVELOPED A PASSION FOR BOXING AT AN EARLY AGE AND BEGAN TRAINING UNDER THE GUIDANCE OF JOE MARTIN. HIS EXCEPTIONAL SKILLS IN THE RING QUICKLY GAINED ATTENTION, LEADING TO A GOLD MEDAL IN THE LIGHT HEAVYWEIGHT DIVISION AT THE 1960 ROME OLYMPICS. INSPIRED BY HIS NEWFOUND SUCCESS, ALI EMBARKED ON A PROFESSIONAL BOXING CAREER THAT WOULD MAKE HIM ONE OF THE GREATEST ATHLETES OF THE 20TH CENTURY.

SUCCESS STORY:

MUHAMMAD ALI'S SUCCESS STORY IS LEGENDARY AND TRANSCENDS THE REALM OF SPORTS. HE BECAME A THREE-TIME WORLD HEAVYWEIGHT CHAMPION AND EARNED A REPUTATION FOR HIS UNPARALLELED CHARISMA, QUICK WIT, AND UNAPOLOGETIC SELF-CONFIDENCE. HE PUBLICLY ANNOUNCED HIS CONVERSION TO ISLAM AND CHANGED HIS NAME TO MUHAMMAD ALI, REFLECTING HIS COMMITMENT TO HIS RELIGIOUS BELIEFS.BEYOND HIS ATHLETIC PROWESS, ALI WAS A CHARISMATIC AND OUTSPOKEN FIGURE ON SOCIAL AND POLITICAL ISSUES. HIS REFUSAL TO BE DRAFTED INTO THE VIETNAM WAR, CITING RELIGIOUS OBJECTIONS AND OPPOSITION TO THE WAR, LED TO HIS SUSPENSION FROM BOXING AND THE STRIPPING OF HIS TITLES. ALI'S LEGACY EXTENDS BEYOND BOXING RINGS. HIS BATTLES INSIDE AND OUTSIDE THE RING, HIS ADVOCACY FOR CIVIL RIGHTS, AND HIS HUMANITARIAN EFFORTS MAKE HIM AN ENDURING CULTURAL ICON.

YESTERDAY · NOW · TOMMOROW

RISE UP

QUOTE

"YOU MAY ENCOUNTER MANY DEFEATS, BUT YOU MUST NOT BE DEFEATED. IN FACT, IT MAY BE NECESSARY TO ENCOUNTER THE DEFEATS, SO YOU CAN KNOW WHO YOU ARE, WHAT YOU CAN RISE FROM, HOW YOU CAN STILL COME OUT OF IT."
— MAYA ANGELOU

RISE UP

QUOTE

"DON'T WAIT FOR SOMEONE TO GREEN-LIGHT YOUR PROJECT, BUILD YOUR OWN INTERSECTION."
- TYLER PERRY

RISE UP

QUOTE

"AS A BLACK ENTREPRENEUR, I REALIZED THAT BUILDING MY OWN
BUSINESS WAS THE ULTIMATE FORM OF EMPOWERMENT."
- URSULA BURNS

RISE UP

QUOTE

"BECOMING A BLACK ENTREPRENEUR ALLOWED ME TO DEFY
STEREOTYPES AND REWRITE THE RULES OF SUCCESS."
- RUSSELL SIMMONS

RISE UP

QUOTE

"FOR BLACK ENTREPRENEURS, EVERY SETBACK IS A SETUP FOR A COMEBACK."
- JOHN HOPE BRYANT

RISE UP

AFFIRMATION

"I LEAD BY EXAMPLE, EMBODYING QUALITIES OF COMPASSION, RESILIENCE, AND DETERMINATION."

RISE UP

QUOTE

"ENTREPRENEURSHIP ALLOWED ME TO TURN MY DREAMS INTO REALITY
AND BUILD A LEGACY FOR FUTURE GENERATIONS."
- OPRAH WINFREY

RISE UP

QUOTE

"AS A BLACK ENTREPRENEUR, I LEARNED THAT PROCRASTINATION
IS THE ENEMY OF PROGRESS; TAKE ACTION NOW, NOT TOMORROW."
- DAYMOND JOHN

RISE UP

QUOTE

"IN THE JOURNEY OF ENTREPRENEURSHIP, THE MOST VALUABLE
CURRENCY IS TIME. DON'T WASTE IT, INVEST IT WISELY."
- URSULA BURNS

RISE UP

QUOTE

"IT'S UP TO YOU TO BRING YOURSELF TO THE ATTENTION OF POWERFUL PEOPLE AROUND YOU. THEY'RE NOT GOING TO FIND YOU ON THEIR OWN."
- RICHARD PARSONS

RISE UP

QUOTE

"OPPORTUNITIES NEVER COME A SECOND TIME, NOR DO THEY
WAIT FOR OUR LEISURE."
- BOOKER T. WASHINGTON

RISE UP

QUOTE

"IN THE WORLD OF ENTREPRENEURSHIP, KNOWLEDGE IS POWER.
AS BLACK ENTREPRENEURS, LET'S EMPOWER OURSELVES THROUGH
CONTINUOUS LEARNING."
- RUSSELL SIMMONS

RISE UP

QUOTE

"AS BLACK ENTREPRENEURS, WE MUST NEVER UNDERESTIMATE THE POWER OF KNOWLEDGE TO UNLOCK DOORS OF OPPORTUNITY."
- JAY-Z

RISE UP

QUOTE

"YOU HAVE TO DEVELOP A HABIT OF DISCIPLINE SO THAT WHEN AN IDEA POPS INTO YOUR HEAD, YOU EXECUTE IT IMMEDIATELY."
- TYLER PERRY

RISE UP

QUOTE

"KNOWLEDGE HAS TO BE IMPROVED, CHALLENGED, AND INCREASED
CONSTANTLY, OR IT VANISHES."
- ALIKO DANGOTE

RISE UP

AFFIRMATION

"I CULTIVATE STRONG RELATIONSHIPS BUILT ON TRUST, RESPECT, AND EMPATHY IN MY ROLE AS A LEADER."

RISE UP

CASE STUDY

MEDGAR EVERS

BACKGROUND:
BORN ON JULY 2, 1925, IN DECATUR, MISSISSIPPI, MEDGAR WAS AN AFRICAN AMERICAN CIVIL RIGHTS ACTIVIST AND FIELD SECRETARY FOR THE MISSISSIPPI CHAPTER OF THE NAACP (NATIONAL ASSOCIATION FOR THE ADVANCEMENT OF COLORED PEOPLE). GROWING UP IN A RACIALLY SEGREGATED AND DISCRIMINATORY ENVIRONMENT, EVERS EXPERIENCED FIRSTHAND THE INJUSTICES FACED BY AFRICAN AMERICANS IN THE SOUTHERN UNITED STATES. AFTER SERVING IN THE U.S. ARMY DURING WORLD WAR II, EVERS BECAME ACTIVELY INVOLVED IN THE CIVIL RIGHTS MOVEMENT, WORKING TO COMBAT RACIAL INEQUALITY.

SUCCESS STORY:
MEDGAR EVERS' SUCCESS STORY IS DEFINED BY HIS UNWAVERING COMMITMENT TO CIVIL RIGHTS AND HIS RELENTLESS PURSUIT OF EQUALITY. AS THE NAACP FIELD SECRETARY IN MISSISSIPPI, EVERS PLAYED A CRUCIAL ROLE IN ORGANIZING CAMPAIGNS AND PROTESTS AGAINST RACIAL SEGREGATION AND VOTER DISENFRANCHISEMENT. HE WORKED TOWARDS DISMANTLING JIM CROW LAWS AND FOUGHT FOR THE RIGHTS OF AFRICAN AMERICANS TO VOTE.
TRAGICALLY, EVERS' LIFE WAS CUT SHORT ON JUNE 12, 1963, WHEN HE WAS ASSASSINATED IN FRONT OF HIS HOME BY A WHITE SUPREMACIST. HIS DEATH BECAME A CATALYST FOR CHANGE, SPARKING INCREASED AWARENESS AND ACTIVISM WITHIN THE CIVIL RIGHTS MOVEMENT. THE TRIAL OF EVERS' MURDERER, BYRON DE LA BECKWITH, RESULTED IN TWO MISTRIALS BEFORE HE WAS FINALLY CONVICTED IN 1994, ILLUSTRATING THE PERSISTENCE REQUIRED TO ACHIEVE JUSTICE IN THE FACE OF RACIAL PREJUDICE.

YESTERDAY - NOW - TOMMOROW

RISE UP

QUOTE

"DISCIPLINE IS THE BRIDGE BETWEEN GOALS & ACCOMPLISHMENT."
- STEVEN BARTLETT

RISE UP

QUOTE

"AS BLACK ENTREPRENEURS, WE HAVE THE POWER TO
REDEFINE NARRATIVES, CREATE WEALTH, AND INSPIRE CHANGE."
- BYRON ALLEN

RISE UP

QUOTE

"EVERY NOW AND THEN YOU HAVE TO NUDGE YOUR PARTNERS.
YOU HAVE TO SPEAK UP AND SPEAK OUT. AND I TRY TO USE
MY PLATFORM FOR THAT. I TRY TO SET AN EXAMPLE."
- ROSALIND BREWER

RISE UP

QUOTE

"WE NEED TO INTERNALIZE THIS IDEA OF EXCELLENCE. NOT MANY FOLKS SPEND A LOT OF TIME TRYING TO BE EXCELLENT."
– BARACK OBAMA

RISE UP

QUOTE

"BEING A BLACK ENTREPRENEUR MEANS TURNING OBSTACLES INTO OPPORTUNITIES AND LIMITATIONS INTO LIMITLESS POTENTIAL."
- SARAH BREEDLOVE (MADAM C.J. WALKER)

RISE UP

QUOTE

"I WORK WITH A LOT OF DRIVEN PEOPLE, AND I FIND THAT, TO BE SUCCESSFUL, YOU HAVE TO BE DISCIPLINED AND YOU HAVE TO BE A TEAM PLAYER. YOU HAVE TO DO YOUR JOB AT A HIGH LEVEL EVERY SINGLE DAY."
- SEAN COMBS

RISE UP

QUOTE

"THE BEST WAY TO NOT FEEL HOPELESS IS TO GET UP AND DO SOMETHING. DON'T WAIT FOR GOOD THINGS TO HAPPEN TO YOU. IF YOU GO OUT AND MAKE SOME GOOD THINGS HAPPEN, YOU WILL FILL THE WORLD WITH HOPE, YOU WILL FILL YOURSELF WITH HOPE."
- BARACK OBAMA

FOR THE BLACK LEADER & BUSINESSMAN

RISE UP

QUOTE

"BEING A BLACK ENTREPRENEUR MEANS EMBRACING CHALLENGES AS OPPORTUNITIES AND TURNING DREAMS INTO REALITIES."
- OPRAH WINFREY

RISE UP

AFFIRMATION

"I AM CAPABLE OF GUIDING OTHERS TOWARDS SUCCESS AND EMPOWERING THEM TO REACH THEIR FULL POTENTIAL."

RISE UP

QUOTE

"ENDEAVOR TO WORK AS HARD AS POSSIBLE TO ATTAIN A NEW AIM WITH EACH DAY THAT COMES BY. DON'T GO TO BED UNTIL YOU HAVE ACHIEVED SOMETHING PRODUCTIVE."
- ALIKO DANGOTE

RISE UP

QUOTE

"THE BATTLES THAT COUNT AREN'T THE ONES FOR GOLD MEDALS. THE STRUGGLES WITHIN YOURSELF—THE INVISIBLE, INEVITABLE BATTLES INSIDE ALL OF US—THAT'S WHERE IT'S AT."
— JESSE OWENS

RISE UP

QUOTE

"THE VERY SERIOUS FUNCTION OF RACISM IS DISTRACTION. IT KEEPS YOU FROM DOING YOUR WORK. IT KEEPS YOU EXPLAINING, OVER AND OVER AGAIN, YOUR REASON FOR BEING."
– TONI MORRISON

RISE UP

QUOTE

"I WANT EVERYBODY TO BE GREAT. YOU KNOW, I'M NOT HATING OR ANYTHING, BUT IT'S A REAL THING. YOU ONLY SEE ONE OR TWO OF US AT A TIME."
- ISSA RAE

RISE UP

QUOTE

"ASSOCIATE YOURSELF WITH PEOPLE OF GOOD QUALITY, FOR IT IS BETTER TO BE ALONE THAN TO BE IN BAD COMPANY."
- BOOKER T. WASHINGTON

RISE UP

QUOTE

"EXCELLENCE IS TO DO A COMMON THING IN AN UNCOMMON WAY. "
- BOOKER T. WASHINGTON

RISE UP

CASE STUDY

BYRON ALLEN

BACKGROUND:

BYRON ALLEN, BORN ON APRIL 22, 1961, IS AN AMERICAN BUSINESSMAN, COMEDIAN, AND MEDIA EXECUTIVE. RAISED IN A LOW-INCOME NEIGHBORHOOD IN DETROIT, MICHIGAN, ALLEN BEGAN HIS CAREER AS A STAND-UP COMEDIAN AT A YOUNG AGE. HIS EARLY EXPERIENCES IN THE ENTERTAINMENT INDUSTRY LAID THE FOUNDATION FOR HIS ENTREPRENEURIAL SPIRIT. IN 1993, HE FOUNDED ENTERTAINMENT STUDIOS.

SUCCESS STORY:

BYRON ALLEN'S SUCCESS STORY IS MARKED BY HIS RESILIENCE, BUSINESS ACUMEN, AND ENTREPRENEURIAL VISION. AFTER ESTABLISHING ENTERTAINMENT STUDIOS, ALLEN STRATEGICALLY EXPANDED THE COMPANY'S REACH AND DIVERSIFIED ITS CONTENT OFFERINGS. INITIALLY FOCUSED ON PRODUCING AND DISTRIBUTING TELEVISION SHOWS, THE COMPANY LATER VENTURED INTO OWNING AND OPERATING CABLE TELEVISION NETWORKS.ONE OF ALLEN'S NOTABLE ACHIEVEMENTS WAS ACQUIRING THE WEATHER CHANNEL IN 2018, A MOVE THAT SOLIDIFIED ENTERTAINMENT STUDIOS AS A SIGNIFICANT PLAYER IN THE MEDIA LANDSCAPE. HIS APPROACH INVOLVES CREATING CONTENT THAT APPEALS TO DIVERSE AUDIENCES, AND HE HAS SUCCESSFULLY DEVELOPED A PORTFOLIO THAT INCLUDES SITCOMS, COURT SHOWS, DOCUMENTARIES, AND MORE.
BYRON ALLEN'S SUCCESS EXTENDS BEYOND ENTERTAINMENT. HE HAS BEEN AN ADVOCATE FOR DIVERSITY AND INCLUSION IN THE MEDIA INDUSTRY, USING HIS POSITION TO ADDRESS ISSUES OF REPRESENTATION AND EQUAL OPPORTUNITIES FOR MINORITIES.

YESTERDAY · NOW · TOMMOROW

RISE UP

QUOTE

"THE HAPPIEST PEOPE ARE THOSE WHO DO THE MOST FOR OTHERS. THE MOST MISERABLE ARE THOSE WHO DO THE LEAST."
- BOOKER T. WASHINGTON

RISE UP

QUOTE

"I WOULDN'T LIMIT MYSELF TO NOTHING. I FEEL LIKE I AM LIMITLESS.
THAT'S THE TRUE MEANING OF BEING A LEADER: BEING ABLE TO DEAL
WITH THE CONSEQUENCES AND TAKE THE RESPONSIBILITY FOR IT. "
- DEVIN BOOKER

FOR THE BLACK LEADER & BUSINESSMAN

RISE UP

AFFIRMATION

"I AM DESTINED TO BE A TRAILBLAZER AND MAKE A MEANINGFUL IMPACT IN MY COMMUNITY."

RISE UP

QUOTE

"GO TO WORK! GO TO WORK IN THE MORN OF A NEW CREATION... UNTIL
YOU HAVE... REACHED THE HEIGHT OFSELF-PROGRESS, AND FROM
THAT PINNACLE BESTOW UPON THE WORLD A CIVILIZATION
OF YOUR OWN."
- MARCUS GARVEY

RISE UP

QUOTE

"GOD AND NATURE FIRST MADE US WHAT WE ARE, AND THEN OUT OF OUR OWN CREATED GENIUS WE MAKE OURSELVES WHAT WE WANT TO BE."
- MARCUS GARVEY

RISE UP

QUOTE

"I WANT TO BE A PART OF PROJECTS THAT CONTRIBUTE TO THE FORWARD MOVEMENT OF BLACK PEOPLE."
- REGINA KING

FOR THE BLACK LEADER & BUSINESSMAN

RISE UP

QUOTE

"A MAN WHO STANDS FOR NOTHING WILL FALL FOR ANYTHING."
- MALCOLM X

RISE UP

QUOTE

"GOD AND NATURE FIRST MADE US WHAT WE ARE, AND THEN OUT OF OUR OWN CREATED GENIUS WE MAKE OURSELVES WHAT WE WANT TO BE."
- MARCUS GARVEY

RISE UP

QUOTE

"THERE IS NO PASSION TO BE FOUND PLAYING SMALL - IN SETTLING FOR A LIFE THAT IS LESS THAN THE ONE YOU ARE CAPABLE OF LIVING."
- NELSON MANDELA

RISE UP

QUOTE

"I PREFER TO BE TRUE TO MYSELF, EVEN AT THE HAZARD OF
INCURRING THE RIDICULE OF OTHERS, RATHER THAN TO BE FALSE,
AND TO INCUR MY OWN ABHORRENCE."
- FREDERICK DOUGLAS

RISE UP

QUOTE

"ALL KIDS NEED IS A LITTLE HELP, A LITTLE HOPE, AND SOMEBODY WHO BELIEVES IN THEM."
- MAGIC JOHNSON

YESTERDAY - NOW - TOMMOROW

RISE UP

QUOTE

"THE ENDS YOU SERVE THAT ARE SELFISH WILL TAKE YOU NO FURTHER THAN YOURSELF, BUT THE ENDS YOU SERVE THAT ARE FOR ALL, IN COMMON, WILL TAKE YOU INTO ETERNITY."
- MARCUS GARVEY

RISE UP

AFFIRMATION

"I HAVE THE COURAGE AND CONFIDENCE TO LEAD WITH
INTEGRITY AND AUTHENTICITY."

RISE UP

QUOTE

"AS A BLACK ENTREPRENEUR, I REALIZED THAT THE ONLY LIMITS TO MY SUCCESS WERE THE ONES I PLACED ON MYSELF."
- TYLER PERRY

RISE UP

QUOTE

"POWER DOESN'T BACK UP IN THE FACE OF A SMILE, OR IN THE FACE OF A THREAT OF SOME KIND OF NONVIOLENT LOVING ACTION. IT'S NOT THE NATURE OF POWER TO BACK UP IN THE FACE OF ANYTHING BUT SOME MORE POWER."
- MINISTER LOUIS FARRAKHAN

RISE UP

QUOTE

"CHANGE WILL NOT COME IF WE WAIT FOR SOME OTHER PERSON OR SOME OTHER TIME. WE ARE THE ONES WE'VE BEEN WAITING FOR. WE ARE THE CHANGE THAT WE SEEK."
- BARACK OBAMA

RISE UP

QUOTE

"IF YOU HAVE NO CRITICS, YOU'LL LIKELY HAVE NO SUCCESS."
- MALCOLM X

RISE UP

CASE STUDY

GARRETT MORGAN

BACKGROUND:
GARRETT AUGUSTUS MORGAN WAS BORN ON MARCH 4, 1877, IN CLAYSVILLE, KENTUCKY. THE SEVENTH OF ELEVEN CHILDREN, MORGAN'S FORMAL EDUCATION WAS LIMITED DUE TO HIS FAMILY'S FINANCIAL CONSTRAINTS. IN 1895, HE MOVED TO CINCINNATI AND THEN LATER TO CLEVELAND, OHIO, WHERE HE WORKED AS A SEWING MACHINE MECHANIC.

SUCCESS STORY:
GARRETT MORGAN'S NOTABLE SUCCESS LIES IN HIS INVENTIVE CONTRIBUTIONS TO TRAFFIC SAFETY AND INDUSTRIAL SAFETY EQUIPMENT. IN 1914, HE PATENTED THE SAFETY HOOD, AN EARLY VERSION OF THE GAS MASK, DESIGNED TO PROTECT INDIVIDUALS FROM INHALING HARMFUL FUMES. THIS INVENTION GAINED ATTENTION DURING A 1916 TUNNEL CONSTRUCTION RESCUE IN CLEVELAND WHEN MORGAN AND HIS BROTHER USED THE SAFETY HOOD TO SAVE WORKERS TRAPPED IN A TUNNEL FILLED WITH NOXIOUS FUMES. MORGAN'S MOST ENDURING LEGACY, HOWEVER, IS THE THREE-POSITION TRAFFIC SIGNAL, PATENTED IN 1923. HIS INNOVATIVE DESIGN INCLUDED A WARNING SIGNAL, ALLOWING DRIVERS TO ANTICIPATE CHANGES IN TRAFFIC LIGHTS, THUS REDUCING ACCIDENTS AT INTERSECTIONS. THE SUCCESS OF THE TRAFFIC SIGNAL LED TO ITS WIDESPREAD ADOPTION IN VARIOUS CITIES, SIGNIFICANTLY IMPACTING ROAD SAFETY

RISE UP

QUOTE

"EDUCATION IS THE MOST POWERFUL WEAPON WHICH YOU CAN USE TO CHANGE THE WORLD. AS BLACK ENTREPRENEURS, LET'S WIELD IT WISELY."
- JOHN HOPE BRYANT

RISE UP

QUOTE

"IF YOU WAKE UP DECIDING WHAT YOU WANT TO GIVE VERSUS WHAT YOU'RE GOING TO GET, YOU BECOME A MORE SUCCESSFUL PERSON. IN OTHER WORDS, IF YOU WANT TO MAKE MONEY, YOU HAVE TO HELP SOMEONE ELSE MAKE MONEY."
— RUSSELL SIMMONS

RISE UP

QUOTE

"THE KEY TO SUCCESS IS NOT JUST IN HAVING A VISION, BUT IN TAKING IMMEDIATE ACTION TOWARDS ITS REALIZATION."
- TYLER PERRY

RISE UP

QUOTE

"EDUCATION IS THE MOST POWERFUL WEAPON WHICH YOU CAN USE TO CHANGE THE WORLD."
- NELSON MANDELA

RISE UP

AFFIRMATION

"I AM COMMITTED TO CONTINUOUS LEARNING AND IMPROVEMENT IN MY LEADERSHIP SKILLS."

RISE UP

QUOTE

"STARTING MY OWN BUSINESS WAS THE BEST DECISION I EVER MADE; IT ALLOWED ME TO CREATE MY OWN PATH TO SUCCESS."
- DAYMOND JOHN

RISE UP

QUOTE

"IF YOU HAVE NO CRITICS, YOU'LL LIKELY HAVE NO SUCCESS."
- MALCOLM X

RISE UP

QUOTE

"STARTING MY OWN BUSINESS WASN'T JUST ABOUT MAKING MONEY, IT WAS ABOUT CREATING OPPORTUNITIES FOR MY COMMUNITY."
- DAYMOND JOHN

RISE UP

QUOTE

"ALMOST ALWAYS, THE CREATIVE DEDICATED MINORITY HAS MADE
THE WORLD BETTER."
– MARTIN LUTHER KING, JR.

RISE UP

QUOTE

"IT ALWAYS SEEMS IMPOSSIBLE UNTIL IT'S DONE."
- NELSON MANDELA

RISE UP

QUOTE

"EXCELLENCE IS THE BEST DETERRENT TO RACISM OR SEXISM."
- OPRAH WINFREY

RISE UP

QUOTE

"I'VE MISSED MORE THAN 9,000 SHOTS IN MY CAREER. I'VE LOST ALMOST 300 GAMES. 26 TIMES, I'VE BEEN TRUSTED TO TAKE THE GAME-WINNING SHOT AND MISSED. I'VE FAILED OVER AND OVER AND OVER AGAIN IN MY LIFE. AND THAT IS WHY I SUCCEED."
- MICHAEL JORDAN

RISE UP

QUOTE

"THE CALMER I AM, THE HIGHER MY SUCCESS RATE. KNOWLEDGE IS
MY BEST ASSET."
- CHRIS GARDNER

FOR THE BLACK LEADER & BUSINESSMAN

RISE UP

QUOTE

"BECOMING A BLACK ENTREPRENEUR ISN'T JUST ABOUT
BREAKING BARRIERS, IT'S ABOUT SHATTERING THEM AND PAVING
THE WAY FOR OTHERS."
- JAY-Z

YESTERDAY - NOW - TOMMOROW

RISE UP

AFFIRMATION

"I EMBRACE MY LEADERSHIP POTENTIAL AND STEP INTO MY POWER TO INSPIRE POSITIVE CHANGE."

RISE UP

CASE STUDY

GEORGE WASHINGTON CARVER

BACKGROUND:
BORN AROUND 1864 IN DIAMOND, MISSOURI, WAS AN AFRICAN AMERICAN AGRICULTURAL SCIENTIST, INVENTOR, AND EDUCATOR. FACING THE CHALLENGES OF SLAVERY DURING HIS EARLY YEARS, CARVER'S RESILIENCE AND PASSION FOR EDUCATION PROPELLED HIM TO IOWA STATE COLLEGE, WHERE HE BECAME THE FIRST AFRICAN AMERICAN TO EARN A BACHELOR OF SCIENCE DEGREE. HE LATER JOINED THE TUSKEGEE INSTITUTE IN ALABAMA, WHERE HE CONDUCTED GROUNDBREAKING RESEARCH IN AGRICULTURAL SCIENCE.

SUCCESS STORY:
GEORGE WASHINGTON CARVER'S SUCCESS STORY LIES IN HIS TRANSFORMATIVE IMPACT ON AGRICULTURAL PRACTICES AND HIS INNOVATIVE APPROACH TO CROP DIVERSIFICATION. AT THE TUSKEGEE INSTITUTE, CARVER ADDRESSED THE AGRICULTURAL CRISIS IN THE SOUTH, CAUSED BY THE OVER-RELIANCE ON COTTON, BY PROMOTING ALTERNATIVE CROPS LIKE PEANUTS, SWEET POTATOES, AND SOYBEANS. HIS WORK SIGNIFICANTLY IMPROVED SOIL QUALITY AND PROVIDED SUSTAINABLE ALTERNATIVES FOR FARMERS.
HIS SUCCESS EXTENDED BEYOND THEORETICAL RESEARCH. HE DEVELOPED OVER 300 PRACTICAL APPLICATIONS FOR PEANUTS, INCLUDING PEANUT BUTTER, OILS, AND VARIOUS PRODUCTS, SHOWCASING THE CROP'S VERSATILITY. THIS NOT ONLY REVITALIZED THE SOUTHERN ECONOMY BUT ALSO REVOLUTIONIZED THE FOOD AND INDUSTRIAL SECTORS. HIS CONTRIBUTIONS TO CROP ROTATION AND SUSTAINABLE FARMING PRACTICES EARNED HIM ACCLAIM AND RECOGNITION.

RISE UP

QUOTE

"EDUCATION IS THE PASSPORT TO THE FUTURE, FOR TOMORROW
BELONGS TO THOSE WHO PREPARE FOR IT TODAY."
- MARTIN LUTHER KING JR

RISE UP

QUOTE

"DISCIPLINE IS THE SOUL OF AN ARMY. IT MAKES SMALL NUMBERS FORMIDABLE; PROCURES SUCCESS TO THE WEAK, AND ESTEEM TO ALL."
- FREDERICK DOUGLASS

RISE UP

QUOTE

"AS BLACK ENTREPRENEURS, WE CAN'T AFFORD TO WAIT FOR THE PERFECT MOMENT. THE TIME IS NOW, TAKE ACTION."
- OPRAH WINFREY

RISE UP

QUOTE

"THE SECRET TO SUCCESS IS TO KNOW SOMETHING NOBODY ELSE KNOWS."
- STEVEN BARTLETT

RISE UP

QUOTE

"EDUCATION IS FOR IMPROVING THE LIVES OF OTHERS AND FOR LEAVING YOUR COMMUNITY AND WORLD BETTER THAN YOU FOUND IT."
- MARIAN WRIGHT EDELMAN

RISE UP

QUOTE

"THE PURPOSE OF EDUCATION IS TO CREATE IN A PERSON THE ABILITY TO LOOK AT THE WORLD FOR HIMSELF, TO MAKE HIS OWN DECISIONS."
- JAMES BALDWIN

RISE UP

QUOTE

"THE BEST WAY TO PREDICT THE FUTURE IS TO CREATE IT."
- URSULA BURNS

FOR THE BLACK LEADER & BUSINESSMAN

RISE UP

QUOTE

"TO ME, WE ARE THE MOST BEAUTIFUL CREATURES IN THE WHOLE WORLD. BLACK PEOPLE. AND I MEAN THAT IN EVERY SENSE."
– NINA SIMONE

RISE UP

AFFIRMATION

"I WELCOME CHALLENGES AS OPPORTUNITIES FOR GROWTH AND DEVELOPMENT AS A LEADER."

RISE UP

QUOTE

"DISCIPLINE IS NOT JUST ABOUT MANAGING YOUR TIME, IT'S ABOUT MANAGING YOUR ENERGY AND YOUR FOCUS TO MAKE THE MOST IMPACT IN YOUR WORK AND PERSONAL LIFE."
- ROBERT SMITH

FOR THE BLACK LEADER & BUSINESSMAN

RISE UP

QUOTE

"I DON'T CARE HOW MUCH POWER, BRILLIANCE, OR ENERGY YOU HAVE, IF YOU DON'T HARNESS IT AND FOCUS IT ON A SPECIFIC TARGET, AND HOLD IT THERE, YOU'RE NEVER GOING TO ACCOMPLISH AS MUCH AS YOUR ABILITY WARRANTS."
- REGINALD LEWIS

RISE UP

QUOTE

"IF THEY DON'T GIVE YOU A SEAT AT THE TABLE, BRING A FOLDING CHAIR."
— SHIRLEY CHISHOLM

RISE UP

QUOTE

"I THINK THE KEY TO SUCCESS IS A COMBINATION OF
BEING DISCIPLINED AND HAVING A CLEAR
VISION OF WHAT YOU WANT."
- RUSSELL SIMMONS

RISE UP

QUOTE

"TIME IS YOUR MOST PRECIOUS COMMODITY. DON'T WASTE IT ON
THINGS THAT DON'T MATTER."
- BOB JOHNSON

RISE UP

QUOTE

"YOUR ENERGY IS GOING TO WHAT YOU SEE VS WHAT YOU SAY. YOUR ENERGY HAS TO MOVE TO WHAT YOU SAY, BECAUSE WHAT YOU SEE WILL NEVER BE THE THE THING YOU WANT."
- MICHAEL IMONITE

RISE UP

QUOTE

"WE CAN TRANSCEND THE SCRIPT OF A PRE-DEFINED STORY, AND
PAVE THE WAY FOR THE FUTURE THAT WE DESIGN.
WE JUST NEED TO TAP THAT POWER, THAT CONVICTION, THAT
DETERMINATION WITHIN US. THE GOOD NEWS IS, WE FOLLOW
PEOPLE THAT LOOK LIKE US IF WE TELL THE STORY THE
RIGHT WAY."
- ROBERT F. SMITH

RISE UP

QUOTE

"WE CAN TRANSCEND THE SCRIPT OF A PRE-DEFINED STORY, AND
PAVE THE WAY FOR THE FUTURE THAT WE DESIGN.
WE JUST NEED TO TAP THAT POWER, THAT CONVICTION, THAT
DETERMINATION WITHIN US. THE GOOD NEWS IS, WE FOLLOW
PEOPLE THAT LOOK LIKE US IF WE TELL THE STORY THE
RIGHT WAY."
- ROBERT F. SMITH

RISE UP

QUOTE

"WE MUST GIVE UP THE SILLY IDEA OF FOLDING OUR HANDS AND WAITING ON GOD TO DO EVERYTHING FOR US. IF GOD HAD INTENDED FOR THAT, THEN HE WOULD NOT HAVE GIVEN US A MIND. WHATEVER YOU WANT IN LIFE, YOU MUST MAKE UP YOUR MIND TO DO IT FOR YOURSELF."
- MARCUS GARVEY

RISE UP

QUOTE

"TIME IS THE MOST VALUABLE ASSET YOU DON'T OWN. YOU MAY OR MAY NOT REALIZE IT YET, BUT HOW YOU USE OR FAIL TO USE YOUR TIME IS GOING TO BE THE BEST INDICATION OF WHERE YOUR FUTURE IS GOING TO TAKE YOU."
- DAYMON JOHN

RISE UP

QUOTE

"CHARACTER, NOT CIRCUMSTANCES, MAKES THE MAN."
- BOOKER T. WASHINGTON

RISE UP

QUOTE

"YOU PRAY FOR RAIN, YOU GOTTA DEAL WITH THE MUD TOO. THAT'S A PART OF IT."
- DENZEL WASHINGTON

RISE UP

QUOTE

"LEARNED THAT COURAGE WAS NOT THE ABSENCE OF FEAR, BUT THE TRIUMPH OVER IT. THE BRAVE MAN IS NOT HE WHO DOES NOT FEEL AFRAID, BUT HE WHO CONQUERS THAT FEAR."
- NELSON MANDELA

RISE UP

QUOTE

"LAUNCHING MY OWN BUSINESS WAS THE MOST CHALLENGING
YET REWARDING JOURNEY I'VE EVER EMBARKED UPON."
- ROBERT L. JOHNSON

FOR THE BLACK LEADER & BUSINESSMAN
RISE UP

SPECIAL DEDICATION:

CKT SOLUTIONS LTD, ESTABLISHED IN 2024, IS A DYNAMIC VENTURE FOUNDED BY THREE ENTREPRENEURS:
CHRISTEVIE TANOE, KRISTAN NEUNIE AND TUNDE BALOGUN.

IT OPERATES UNDER AN UMBRELLA OF ADVOCACY AND POSITIVE IMPACT WITH A SPECIFIC FOCUS ON CULTIVATING TOMORROW'S BLACK LEADERS. THE CORE SERVICES ENCOMPASS A BROAD SPECTRUM, INCLUDING DIGITAL MARKETING AND FUNDRAISING. THE OVERARCHING GOAL IS TO LEVERAGE THE PLATFORM TO GENERATE WEALTH AND, IN TURN, CONTRIBUTE TO THE EMPOWERMENT OF THE BLACK COMMUNITY. THE COMPANY IS COMMITTED TO PROVIDING INCREASED OPPORTUNITIES FOR BLACK ENTREPRENEURS AND AIMS TO MAKE A LASTING IMPACT BY OFFERING MENTORING AND GUIDANCE THROUGH SOCIAL MEDIA CHANNELS. OVERALL, CKT EMBODIES A HOLISTIC APPROACH, BLENDING BUSINESS SUCCESS WITH A STRONG COMMITMENT TO SOCIAL RESPONSIBILITY AND COMMUNITY DEVELOPMENT.

HERE IS WHAT THEY HAD TO SAY...

"EVERYTHING IN LIFE IS MINDSET. YOU CAN GIVE A BLANK PAPER TO ONE PERSON AND £100 TO ANOTHER BUT THE RETURN WOULD BE DIFFERENT."
- CHRISTIVIE TANOE

"IF YOU MAKE SMALL CONSISTENT CHANGES TO YOUR LIFE, EVERYONE WILL SOON RECOGNISE THE BIG CHANGE IN YOUR FORTUNE."
- KRISTAN NEUNIE

"THERE ARE FEW BETTER PERSONAL SATISFACTION THAN LOOKING IN THE MIRROR KNOWING YOU GAVE IT EVERYTHING. THAT MIXED WITH WANTING TO MAKE DIFFERENCE IN THE WORLD, IS A COMBINATION THAT MAKES DREAMS COME TRUE."
- TUNDE BALOGUN

CKT
SOLUTIONS

YESTERDAY - NOW - TOMMOROW